Computers
Then and Now

by Rebecca Weber

Content Adviser: Brian VanVoorst,
Principal Research Scientist, Honeywell Labs

Reading Adviser: Rosemary G. Palmer, Ph.D.,
Department of Literacy, College of Education,
Boise State University

Spyglass
BOOKS

COMPASS POINT BOOKS
Minneapolis, Minnesota

Compass Point Books
3109 West 50th Street, #115
Minneapolis, MN 55410

Visit Compass Point Books on the Internet at *www.compasspointbooks.com*
or e-mail your request to *custserv@compasspointbooks.com*

Photographs ©: Gary Sundermeyer, cover (bottom); Bettmann/Corbis, cover background, 7;
DigitalVision, 5; Hulton/Archive by Getty Images, 9, 11, 13; Scholastic Studio 10/Index Stock Imagery,
15; LWA–JDC/Corbis, 17; Forestier Yves/Corbis Sygma, 19; PhotoDisc, 20, 21.

Creative Director: Terri Foley
Managing Editor: Catherine Neitge
Editor: Jennifer VanVoorst
Photo Researcher: Svetlana Zhurkina
Designer: Les Tranby
Educational Consultant: Diane Smolinski

Library of Congress Cataloging-in-Publication Data
Weber, Rebecca.
 Computers then and now / Rebecca Weber.
  v. cm. — (Spyglass books)
 Includes bibliographical references and index.
 Contents: Living with computers—Early machines—The first computers—
 Home computers—Inventing the internet—Computers of the future—Bits and pieces.
 ISBN 0-7565-0654-9 (hardcover)
 1. Computers-–Juvenile literature. [1. Computers.] I. Title. II. Series.
 QA76.23W43 2004
 004—dc22   2003024099

ISBN 0-7565-1054-6 First printing in paperback, 2005

Contents

NOTE: Glossary words are in **bold** the first time they appear.

Living with Computers

Computers are a big part of our lives. We play computer games. Even cars and clocks have computers.

We haven't always had computers to help us, though.

Early Machines

Hundreds of years ago, people began building machines that could solve problems. One of the earliest of these machines was built in 1642. It could add and subtract.

In 1801, a factory owner built the first machine that used *punch cards.* The machine's needles followed the holes in the cards to weave patterns.

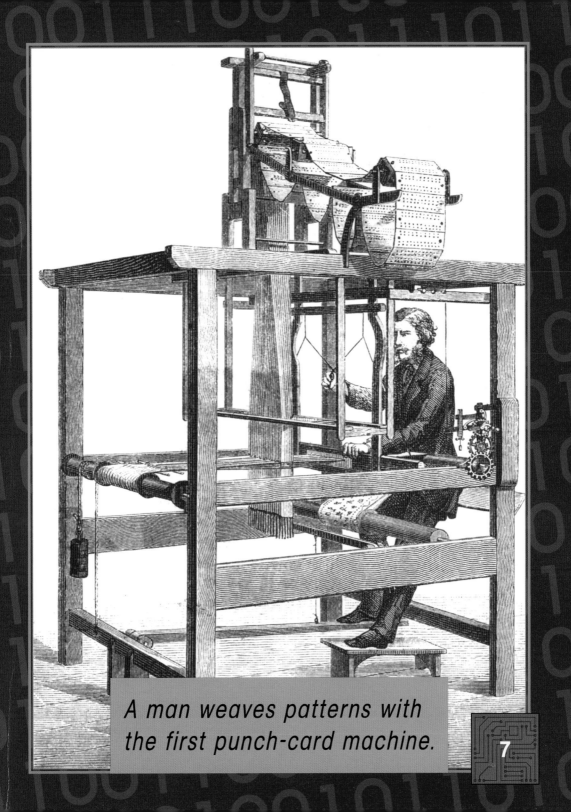

A man weaves patterns with the first punch-card machine.

In 1888, an American inventor named Herman Hollerith built a punch-card machine to do addition for the U.S. *census.*

Hollerith started a company that today is called IBM.

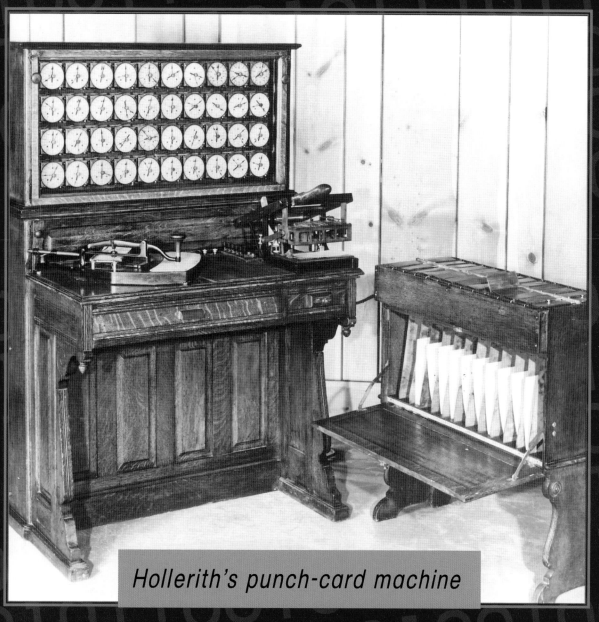

Hollerith's punch-card machine

The First Computers

Inventions in the early 1900s gave these machines even more abilities. Many companies began to make these machines, now called computers.

These early computers cost a lot of money. They were also very large. Even just 30 years ago, most computers were larger than a two-car garage!

A large computer from the 1960s

In the early 1970s, though, *scientists* learned how to put all of a computer's information on small *chips.*

These chips helped scientists make computers smaller. Computers were also becoming more powerful. They cost less money, too.

A computer chip from 1974

Home Computers

The first computer small enough to be used in the home became available in 1975. It was not very powerful, though. It could only run one *program* at a time.

Today, some computers can fit in the palm of your hand. These computers are even more powerful than the computers that were garage-sized!

14

A handheld computer

Inventing the Internet

In 1969, scientists linked four computers together to share information. This was the beginning of the *Internet.*

By the 1990s, people started hooking up their home computers to the Internet.

Today, people all around the world use the Internet.

Computers of the Future

Scientists are still working to make computers smaller and more powerful. Some scientists are working to make computers that people can wear.

Computers have come a long way! What do you think computers will be like when you grow up?

A wearable computer

19

Bits and Pieces

- Computers store all of their information using the numbers 1 and 0. A 1 or a 0 is called a bit. The different groupings of these bits can make any kind of word, picture, or sound.

- There are more computers built into everyday things like dishwashers and cars than there are home computers.

- Most computer chips are made out of a material called *silicon.* This is the same thing that sand is made of.

Glossary

census–a count of how many people live in a country

chips–small, thin slices of special material that contain a large number of electronic parts

Internet–a set of hundreds of millions of computers connected to share information

program–something that uses a computer's power to do work

punch cards–cards that have holes punched in them to make a machine do something

scientists–people who work to solve problems and learn about the world

silicon–a chemical element found in sand

Learn More

Books

Roza, Greg. *The Incredible Story of Computers and the Internet.* New York: PowerKids Press, 2004.

Worland, Gayle. *The Computer.* Mankato, Minn.: Capstone Press, 2004.

On the Web

For more information on **Computers Then and Now,** use FactHound to track down Web sites related to this book.

1. Go to **www.facthound.com**
2. Type in a search word related to this book or this book ID: 0756506549.
3. Click on the **Fetch It** button.

Your trusty FactHound will fetch the best Web sites for you!

Index

GR: L
Word Count: 321

From Rebecca Weber

Whenever I travel to a new place, I enjoy learning about people and their daily lives. I hope this book opens up a little bit of the world for you!

24